NATIONAL
GEOGRAPHIC

From Field to Florist

Felix James

FLOWER STORE

Look at the flowers.
They are for sale
in a flower store.

2

A person who sells flowers is called a florist. Where does the florist get all the flowers?

Farmers grow the flowers.

Some of the flowers are grown in large fields.

Some of the flowers are grown in greenhouses.

In the morning, farmers pick the flowers they will sell at the market.

They put the flowers in their truck.

They take their flowers to the market.

At the market the flowers are kept in buckets full of water.
The water helps keep the flowers fresh.

8

Florists visit the market.
This is where they get the flowers
to sell in their stores.

9

The florist gets the flowers ready to sell at the store. Some of the flowers are made up into bunches.

People buy flowers
at the flower store.

11

From Field to Florist

Flowers
grow

Flowers at
the market

Flowers at
the store

People buy
flowers